The Clouds, Mother Earth and the Space Between

Shahram Khosraviani

The Clouds, Mother Earth and the Space Between

CONTENTS

To my children: Margaux, Persia, Lilee and Naveed

As you journey through this world, with all its wonders and challenges, remember to also turn your gaze inward. The answers you seek, the strength you need, the love you crave – they all reside within you. You are a wellspring of power, capable of incredible things. You are a beacon of love, radiating warmth and compassion to those around you. And you possess a unique and radiant beauty, both inside and out.

Trust the whispers of your intuition, the wisdom of your heart.

Believe in the magic that slumbers within your soul, waiting to be awakened. You have the power to shape your reality, to manifest your dreams, and to create a life filled with joy, purpose, and authentic connection.

Shahram Khosraviani's *The Clouds, Mother Earth and the Space Between* is more than just a memoir; it's an intimate journey alongside the author as he navigates the complexities of life. Khosraviani doesn't shy away from vulnerability, openly exploring his personal struggles with identity formation, the search for self-worth, and the pursuit of genuine happiness.

But what truly sets this book apart is its interactive approach. Khosraviani masterfully weaves **reflective prompts** throughout the narrative, transforming the reading experience into a dynamic conversation. At the end of each chapter, these carefully crafted prompts encourage introspection, urging readers to delve into their own experiences and connect with the themes on a deeper level. It's like having a personal journal integrated within the book, guiding readers towards self-discovery and a more profound understanding of their own lives.

By sharing his own story and providing these insightful prompts, Khosraviani empowers readers to embark on their own journeys of self-reflection, making *The Clouds, Mother Earth and the Space Between* a unique and transformative reading experience.

1

The Sky & The Stars

Shahram's formative years were spent in a bustling household shared with his aunt, her family, and his grandparents. Some of his most cherished childhood recollections involve strolling to school alongside his uncle, engaging in playful games with neighborhood friends, immersing himself in comic books on Sundays, enjoying quality time with his sister, and taking leisurely walks in the park with his grandmother.

Sometimes, he'd find himself captivated by the ever-shifting shapes of the clouds. At night, his gaze would turn upwards, drawn to the celestial spectacle above. He'd sit back, mesmerized by the twinkling stars, his imagination running wild with tales of life on those distant celestial bodies. Stargazing became a cherished pastime, a source of endless wonder and inspiration.

A persistent question lingered in the back of his mind, surfacing from time to time to prick at his curiosity and stir a sense of confusion. It was a simple yet profound question: why wasn't his dad living with him?

Though his father was largely absent from his daily life, he maintained a connection through weekly phone calls and yearly visits that typically lasted a few weeks. The anticipation of these visits filled him with a childlike excitement, a joyous countdown to the precious time he would spend with his dad. Those weeks were filled with laughter, shared adventures, and a sense of closeness that temporarily filled the void of his father's absence.

His father's departures were heart-wrenching, leaving Shahram feeling abandoned and confused. This inconsistent presence only deepened his longing for a father and his curiosity about his absence.

After his dad left, Shahram would kind of shut down for a few days and let the sadness wash over him. He got really good at hiding his feelings and putting on a happy face, even though he was hurting inside. It was his way of coping and dealing with the questions he had about his dad. Moments like receiving his school report card, with its empty "Parent" section, pierced Shahram's facade, reminding him of his father's absence and his longing for his presence and approval.

Over time, Shahram learned about his father's life - his remarriage, financial struggles, and move to a new country. Understanding these circumstances, though tinged with sadness, helped him make sense of his father's absence.

Shahram's journey of understanding and acceptance led him to a profound realization: love, in its many forms, is a beautiful and powerful force. He learned that love isn't confined to the traditional family structure but can blossom in unexpected places. The love he received from his extended family, despite the absence of his parents, taught him the importance of embracing the love that surrounds us, even if it comes in unconventional ways.

Moreover, Shahram discovered the transformative power of acceptance. By accepting his circumstances, he was able to move beyond bitterness and resentment. Acceptance paved the way for healing and allowed him to appreciate the love that was present in his life, fostering a sense of gratitude and contentment.

Self Reflecting

- How do I define love? What does it mean to me?
- Has my understanding of love evolved over time?
- How freely do I give and receive love in my life?
- In what situations or contexts do I find love most present or relevant?
- In what ways does love enrich my life currently?
- Are there any ways in which love is currently hindering or holding me back?
- When has love been a source of pain or disappointment in my past?
- What are some of the biggest misconceptions or myths about love that I've encountered?
- What are my greatest fears and hopes when it comes to love?
- How do I envision love positively impacting my future?

2

The Inheritance of Absence

Shahram's childhood was marked by the conspicuous absence of his father, a void that fueled a relentless stream of self-doubt and questioning. Initially, he clung to the simple explanation that his father worked in a different city, a plausible reason for his physical distance. However, as time passed and the reality of his father's minimal involvement sunk in, this comforting narrative crumbled.

In its place, a toxic seed of self-blame took root. Shahram, unable to fathom any other explanation, internalized his father's absence as a personal rejection. He convinced himself that he was somehow unworthy of love, that his own shortcomings were the reason his father chose to remain distant.

The pity and outpouring of love from his family and relatives inadvertently reinforced Shahram's belief that love was something to be earned through compliance and agreeability. He equated kindness with affection, assuming that if he was consistently pleasant and accommodating, others would naturally reciprocate with love.

Though loved by his family, Shahram's father's absence fueled self-doubt, making him question his father's love and his own worth. This distorted his view of relationships and trapped him in a cycle of self-blame, as he remained unaware of the true reasons for his father's absence.

Internalized guilt and shame from his father's absence drove Shahram to prioritize kindness and agreeability, believing his worthiness of love depended on his behavior. He became a people-pleaser, constantly seeking validation.

Shahram's need for validation led him to constantly agree with others, even when he disagreed, to avoid conflict and maintain a sense of acceptance. This suppression of his own needs became so ingrained that he lost sight of its origins in his childhood wounds.

Shahram's pattern of seeking validation continued through adolescence, leading him to suppress his true feelings and agree with others even when he disagreed. This constant self-betrayal eroded his sense of self and left him feeling unfulfilled in relationships built on unspoken resentments.

As Shahram matured, he observed how others asserted their needs without fear of losing love, contrasting with his own struggle to say "no." This prompted him to examine his past, realizing that his father's absence and the pity he received from relatives led him to internalize the belief that love was conditional and earned through compliance.

Realizing his people-pleasing stemmed from a fear of rejection, Shahram began reclaiming his autonomy. He started expressing his true feelings and setting boundaries, gradually liberating himself despite moments of self-doubt.

Shahram discovered that expressing his needs and setting boundaries didn't jeopardize genuine love, but rather strengthened relationships. This realization empowered him to embrace his authentic self, shed his people-pleasing tendencies, and overcome his fear of rejection.

Self Reflecting

- What does self-worth mean to me?
- How would I describe my current level of self-worth?
- What are my strengths and weaknesses?
- What are some past experiences that have influenced my self-worth?
- How do my thoughts and beliefs affect my self-worth?
- Who are the people whose opinions matter most to me, and why?
- In what ways do I compare myself to others, and how does that affect my self-worth?
- What are some things I can do to cultivate a stronger sense of self-worth?
- How can I challenge and overcome my self-doubt?
- How would my life be different if I had unshakeable self-worth?

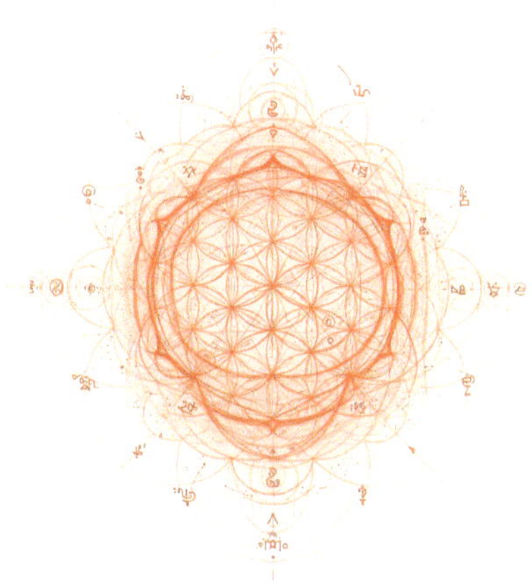

3

Chasing the Sun, Finding the Light

Shahram's early years were filled with love and support from his family, so he felt safe and secure, and unlike many kids, he wasn't afraid of the dark. He was totally comfortable at night, whether it was with a nightlight or those motion-sensor lights that would flash on and off. He had a real sense of confidence as a kid, thanks to the loving home he grew up in.

Out of nowhere, Shahram was hit with intense anxiety. It was like this awful feeling of uncertainty and helplessness that just wouldn't go away. He felt okay during the day, but as soon as it started to get dark, he'd be terrified of having another panic attack. He even had this crazy thought that if he could fly west and chase the sun, he could avoid the night and the anxiety that came with it!

Desperate to escape the nighttime panic attacks, Shahram fantasized about chasing the sun. He'd take long bike rides at dusk, then brace himself for the inevitable panic in his room with calming music. Each night, he'd erupt, turning on every light and pacing frantically, leaving his family feeling helpless. The relentless cycle of panic attacks was exhausting and isolating.

Concerned about Shahram's debilitating panic attacks, his family sought advice. A wise family friend, Uncle Tah, suggested a different approach: instead of battling his anxiety, Shahram should try to understand it. He likened it to befriending the anxiety, encouraging him to explore its triggers, patterns, and underlying causes, as if solving a mystery within himself. This insightful advice marked the beginning of Shahram's journey toward healing.

Embracing his new approach, Shahram faced his next panic attack by sitting in the dark and conversing with his fear. He acknowledged its protective intent but asserted his independence. He repeated this over several nights, sometimes gently, sometimes with anger, growing more confident each time. Finally, a profound shift occurred: a strange sensation in his chest signaled the fear's departure, leaving him with a newfound sense of peace and control.

Shahram smiled, his heart full. He had learned that true bravery wasn't about running away from fear, but about facing it, understanding it, and ultimately, befriending it. He knew that life would always have its challenges, but he also knew that he had the strength within himself to handle them.

He had the love and support of his family, a love that had always been there, a constant source of light that helped him find his way back from the darkness. And now, more than ever, he was filled with hope, a deep and abiding hope for a future filled with peaceful nights and bright tomorrows, a future he was no longer afraid to embrace. He looked up at the starlit sky, a sense of peace washing over him.

He was home, truly home, in the comforting embrace of the night, his heart full of love, gratitude, and an unshakeable hope for all the days to come.

Self Reflecting

- What does emotional well-being mean to me?
- How would I describe my overall emotional state currently?
- What are my most common emotional triggers?
- How do I typically respond to these triggers?
- What are some healthy ways I express my emotions?
- What are my go-to strategies for dealing with stress and difficult emotions?
- What practices or activities help me regulate my emotions and maintain inner peace?
- How do I cultivate positive emotions like joy, gratitude, and compassion?
- Who are the people I turn to for emotional support?
- What are some areas where I can improve my emotional well-being?

4 |

From Pleasing to Peace

Shahram had a pretty typical, happy childhood. He loved hanging out with his family and friends, but he was also a deep thinker who liked to watch people. He'd spend hours on his balcony just observing the world go by. It fascinated him how people interacted with each other. He'd watch his family, friends, and even total strangers, and then he'd replay those interactions in his head, thinking about how he would have acted in those situations. He was always trying to understand people better.

Shahram had a great family who taught him all about love and empathy. But even though he had that strong foundation, he still felt the pressure to have that "perfect" life—you know, the amazing job, the perfect spouse, the whole nine yards. It made him feel kind of stressed and confused, like he had to live up to some impossible standard.

Shahram was raised with a lot of love and was a keen observer of people, so he thought he was basically figuring out the formula for a perfect life. He imagined himself handling every situation with total confidence, getting everything he wanted, and being exactly what society expected. But deep down, he was afraid no one would ever truly love him enough to want to be with him.

He was obsessed with being perfect, so he tried to use his "perfect" solutions for every situation in his life. He planned out every interaction and decision, convinced that his way was the only way to succeed. But when things didn't go according to plan (which, let's be real, happens all the time!), he'd beat himself up about it and feel like a total failure. This just made him more insecure and convinced him that he wasn't good enough.

Shahram was really hard on himself when things went wrong. He'd blame himself for not predicting every possible outcome, which is impossible! He was always overthinking everything and putting everyone else's needs first, because he really wanted to love and be loved. But all of that took a toll on him. He felt exhausted and unsure of himself, like he was stuck in this pattern and didn't know how to break free.

Shahram noticed that his friends didn't seem to stress as much as he did. They just said what they wanted without worrying about what other people thought, and it didn't seem to affect their friendships at all. This made Shahram rethink everything. He always thought that love meant putting other people first, but seeing his friends be more direct made him wonder if he had it all wrong. It even made him question if some people were just using others to get what they wanted.

Shahram felt totally stuck. He wanted to stop putting everyone else first, but it felt wrong to focus on his own needs. He was raised to always think of others, and his family always put him first, especially his aunt. He remembered how she'd sleep on the floor when he was sick or stay in the hospital with him, even sleeping in a chair.

Shahram started to realize that his idea of always putting others first wasn't how everyone else operated, especially when everyone was telling him to go after his own "perfect" life. So he decided to try something wild: saying "no." He started small, but even the thought of saying "no" to someone made him super anxious. Finally, he actually did it! He said "no." It felt like a huge deal, like he was breaking some unspoken rule. He was so nervous that he actually closed his eyes and crossed his fingers, hoping he didn't ruin the relationship or hurt the other person's feelings.

Shahram was shocked! The person he said "no" to was totally cool with it. They didn't get mad or upset; they just accepted it and moved on. Shahram was so relieved. He had finally put himself first, and nothing bad happened!

That initial "no" was merely the first step in a long journey of self-discovery and liberation. Shahram realized that he needed to carefully unravel the intricate tapestry of "lessons" woven into his childhood, replacing them with a newfound understanding of his own worth and needs. The process was slow and deliberate, requiring him to cultivate a deeper intimacy with his own feelings and desires. He began to recognize that consistently placing others' needs above his own had not only led to personal exhaustion but also fostered a subtle resentment that threatened to erode his relationships over time.

As he gradually learned to set healthy boundaries, Shahram discovered a profound sense of ease and inner peace. He no longer felt the constant pressure to please everyone or anticipate their every need. This newfound freedom filled his heart with a genuine happiness and joy that radiated outwards, positively impacting his interactions with others. People were drawn to his authenticity and self-assurance, creating a more balanced and fulfilling dynamic in his relationships.

Self Reflecting

- Who am I?
- What are my core values and beliefs?
- What are my strengths and weaknesses?
- What are my passions and dreams?
- What am I grateful for in my life?
- What are my biggest fears and insecurities?
- How do I react to challenges and setbacks?
- What are my patterns in relationships with others?
- What are my goals and aspirations for the future?
- What is the legacy I want to leave behind?

From Obligation to Authenticity

Shahram, a creature of habit, found his rigid routines increasingly suffocating. He felt trapped, fearing that any change would disappoint those around him. This internal conflict – the desire to please versus the yearning for authenticity – gnawed at him. He longed for freedom but remained a prisoner of his own making, a martyr to his routines.

This struggle extended to his friendships as well. He realized that a particular friendship had become draining, a mismatch of personalities and desires. Though comfortable and familiar, it no longer brought him joy. Determined to prioritize his own well-being, Shahram bravely chose to end the friendship. He began distancing himself, creating space and prioritizing his own needs, despite the awkwardness and the fear of letting go.

Shahram started pulling away from the friendship, saying no to things, keeping phone calls short, and generally creating some distance. It was a bit awkward, but he was determined to put himself first.

At first, it felt weird not hanging out with his friend anymore. It was like having a blank space in his life where that friendship used to be. He felt a bit lost and unsure what to do with himself.

But then, instead of finding someone else to fill that space, Shahram started paying attention to what he wanted. He rediscovered old hobbies, tried new things, and just did what he felt like doing, not what he felt he should be doing. It was a really cool moment for him.

A sense of liberation washed over him, a lightness he hadn't felt in years. The energy that had once been drained by a forced connection was now flowing freely, fueling his creativity and passion. He felt more alive, more aligned with his true self.

This inner transformation rippled outwards, affecting his interactions with others. He approached relationships with a newfound authenticity, offering kindness and support from a place of genuine love, not obligation. His heart opened wider, and he found himself connecting with people on a deeper, more meaningful level.

Breaking free from that stagnant routine had been a catalyst, a turning point in Shahram's journey. It had taught him the importance of honoring his own needs, of choosing growth over comfort, and of defining relationships on his own terms. He had discovered that true connection comes from a place of authenticity, not obligation, and that letting go of the old can create space for something truly beautiful to blossom.

Self Reflecting

- What does authenticity mean to me?[
- What does it mean to live a life true to yourself?
- How has my understanding of authenticity evolved over time?
- How comfortable are you sharing your true thoughts and feelings with others?
- How do you show up authentically in your relationships with friends, family, and romantic partners?
- Do you feel like you can be authentic in your workplace or creative field?
- How do you handle situations where your authenticity might clash with the expectations of others?
- What are some internal or external barriers that prevent me from being more authentic?
- What steps can you take to become more authentic?
- How can you embrace your strengths and vulnerabilities authentically?

6

Beyond the Ranking

Shahram grew up enveloped in love, his childhood a haven of warmth and acceptance. He floated through his days with an untroubled spirit, his world a canvas of vibrant colors and joyful experiences. He reveled in playtime adventures, cherished moments with his family, the camaraderie of friends, and the exciting novelty of school.

Then fifth grade arrived, and suddenly grades were a thing. At first, Shahram wasn't worried. He was a good student and figured he'd do great. But when he got his first test back, he was crushed. He was average, right in the middle of the class.

He became determined to get back to being "perfect." He studied harder than ever, trying to get the best grades in the class. He hated the idea of being ranked against other students. It just didn't make sense to him. He had fleeting thought that everyone was perfect in their own way, so why did they have to be compared and categorized?

As Shahram grew older, this habit of comparing himself to others stuck with him. It felt like he always had to prove himself, not just in school, but in life in general. It was exhausting! it wasn't just about grades anymore. Now, Shahram felt pressure to have the best job, the biggest house, the latest gadgets —all that stuff that society says makes you successful. It was exhausting!

It was like he traded in a happy childhood where he could just be himself for a grown-up life where everyone was judging him based on his stature, his job, and his material possessions.

It finally hit him how pointless this whole competition was. The need to compete started from the moment you were born and messed with how you saw yourself and the world. It was like a big lie everyone believed that stole your peace and made you feel like you weren't good enough unless you had certain things or achieved certain things.

This was a big wake-up call for Shahram. He started questioning all those rules about what makes a person successful. He wanted to find his own way and be happy with who he was, flaws and all. There's no such thing as perfect. True happiness comes from enjoying the journey, even with all its ups and downs, and not getting hung up on some impossible ideal.

This was a huge relief for Shahram. He didn't have to compare himself to others anymore or worry about what other people thought. He knew his life was his own unique adventure, and that was awesome!

He finally understood that trying to impress others wouldn't make him happy. True happiness came from being himself and doing what he loved. It was like a weight had been lifted off his shoulders.

Shahram discovered that true happiness wasn't about achieving a flawless facade, but about embracing the messy, imperfect, and utterly beautiful reality of his own life. It was about finding joy in the everyday moments, in the pursuit of his passions, and in the connections he forged with others. It was about living a life that felt meaningful and fulfilling, not because it met society's standards, but because it resonated with the deepest desires of his heart.

Self Reflecting

- What does true happiness mean to you?
- What are the key ingredients of true happiness in your life?
- Is true happiness is an achievable goal or an ongoing journey?
- What are moments in your life when you felt truly happy?
- What are you doing now that brings you happiness?
- What are some obstacles that prevent you from happiness?
- Has your definition of true happiness evolved over time?
- Do you believe everyone has the potential to experience true happiness?
- What is the relationship between true happiness and things like success, wealth, and material possessions?
- What is the ultimate purpose of pursuing true happiness?

Shahram's journey is a tale of self-discovery.

Raised to equate his worth with external success, he falls into a pattern of seeking validation and suppressing his true self.

As he matures, he questions these beliefs and embarks on a path of embracing his authenticity, learning to set boundaries and prioritize his own needs. Through this process, he discovers that true happiness lies in self-acceptance and genuine connection, not external validation.

This book invites readers to join Shahram's transformative journey toward inner peace and the freedom of living authentically.

Love you for who you are - life is beautiful without the lens we are accustomed to wear - shine on - you're beautiful